ICE HOCKEY LEGENDS

Wayne Gretzky

Brett Hull

Jaromir Jagr

Mario Lemieux

Eric Lindros

Mark Messier

CHELSEA HOUSE PUBLISHERS

ICE HOCKEY LEGENDS

JAROMIR JAGR

Dean Schabner

CHELSEA HOUSE PUBLISHERS

Philadelphia

Produced by Daniel Bial and Associates
New York, New York

Picture research by Alan Gottlieb
Cover illustration by Earl Parker

First Printing

1 3 5 7 9 8 6 4 2

Library of Congress Cataloging-in-Publication Data

Schabner, Dean
     Jaromir Jagr / Dean Schabner.
        p.   cm. — (Ice hockey legends)
     Includes bibliographical references (p.) and index.
     Summary: The life story of the Czechoslovakian-born hockey player
for the Pittsburgh Penguins who is one of the most talented and
promising players in the National Hockey League.
     ISBN 0-7910-4556-0
     1. Jagr, Jaromir. 1972–   —Juvenile literature.   2. Hockey
players—Czech Republic—Biography—Juvenile literature.   [1. Jagr,
Jaromir, 1972–   .   2. Hockey players.]   I. Title.   II. Series.
GV848.5.J35S35   1997
796.962'092—dc21
     [B]   97-30870
                                                                          CIP
                                                                          AC

CONTENTS

MARIO JR.

The Pittsburgh Penguins were in a terrible fix. It was the spring of 1992 and the defending National Hockey League champions were trying to get back to the Stanley Cup finals, but they were going to have to do it without their biggest star, Mario Lemieux. Super Mario, as he was called because of his blinding speed and unstoppable power, was out with a broken hand—an injury he suffered when Adam Graves of the New York Rangers slashed him across the hands with his stick in the third game of the second-round series.

If the Penguins were going to get past the Rangers, the team that had run up the best record in the NHL during the regular season, Jaromir Jagr, the 20-year-old from Czechoslovakia known as Mario Jr., was going to have to prove his nickname had more to do with hock-

Jaromir Jagr was a one-man wrecking crew when the Pittsburgh Penguins faced the New York Rangers in the 1992 playoffs.

7

ey than with his looks and the coincidental combination of letters in his first name.

The Rangers were an experienced squad, built in the character of their captain, Mark Messier, the tough, wily veteran of four championship teams. And they had the home ice advantage— the seven-game series was tied at two games apiece, but two of the final three contests would be played in New York.

Jagr had already established himself as one of the best young players in hockey. If anything, Jagr was quicker than Lemieux—a player he had idolized since seeing him playing for Canada in a junior tournament when Jagr was just a boy. Penguin opponents had become familiar with the mop of curly dark hair that hung out from the back of Jagr's helmet, because often that was all they saw as Jagr left them behind, racing toward the net with the puck on his stick. But he had yet to prove he had Lemieux's ability to perform when his teammates needed him most.

Jagr was among the first of a wave of players from Eastern Europe to enter the NHL as the Iron Curtain created by the communist regime in the Soviet Union began to be pushed aside. He had the flash and the speed the Europeans were known for, and if he was ever going to end the myth that the Czechs and Russians could not stand the physical punishment that gets dished out in the NHL playoffs, this was the perfect time.

The Penguins made a statement early in that Game 5 in New York. Just 1:15 into the game, Rick Tocchet took a perfect cross-ice pass from Ron Francis and scored to give Pittsburgh a 1-0 lead. Six minutes later, Jagr got his first chance. Rangers defenseman Brian Leetch pulled him down to stop him from charging in alone on goalie John Vanbiesbrouck, but the referee whistled Leetch for the assault and gave Jagr a penalty shot—a one-on-one opportunity against the goalie. That was exactly what Leetch had been trying to prevent. Without the help of a defenseman to slow down Jagr, Vanbiesbrouck did not have a prayer of stopping the young Penguin, and as quickly as that, Pittsburgh had a 2–0 lead in what would likely be the deciding game in the series.

The Rangers were not finished, though. Vanbiesbrouck and New York's tough defense closed the door on the Penguins while Darren Turcotte and Mike Gartner both scored to tie the score by early in the third period. As time ticked away, the game seemed to have swung the Rangers' way. They were getting more shots on Pittsburgh goalie Tom Barrasso than they were allowing, and the Madison Square Garden crowd was roaring at every opportunity that their team got.

With less than six minutes left, Jagr silenced them. He controlled a pass at the Rangers' blue line. He was met by burly Jeff Beukeboom, but deked the Ranger defenseman and left him to watch, open-mouthed like the 19,000 fans in the stands, as he cut in alone on Vanbiesbrouck for the second time that night. Whatever the Ranger goalie had learned in the first meeting that night was worthless to him now. Jagr sent Vanbiesbrouck sprawling with a devilish fake, then flipped the puck into the open net.

Mario Jr., who would go on to score the winning goal in Game 6, had lived up to his nickname.

THE PRAGUE SPRING

Perhaps the most significant event in Jaromir Jagr's life occurred four years before he was born, when Soviet tanks rolled into Czechoslovakia to put an icy end to what was known as the Prague Spring. All over the world, 1968 was a year of youthful revolt in the name of freedom. Students took to the streets of Paris, and all across America there were sit-ins, love-ins, and be-ins, as young people sought to force their elders to change.

What happened in Czechoslovakia was just the opposite, though. In January, a man named Alexander Dubcek became the leader of the nation, ousting a hard-line communist. Dubcek had been a World War II hero, fighting in the communist underground against the Germans. Now he wanted to replace the stern form of government imposed on Czechoslovakia by the Soviet Union with what he called "socialism with a human face."

In 1968, youths demonstrated in Prague's Wenceslas Square supporting the less restrictive Communist government.

All the things that young people were fighting for in other countries, Dubcek put in place in Czechoslovakia. He stopped censorship, encouraged the arts, and allowed newspapers to open and express whatever views they wanted to. He even threw open a cautious window to the West. The Soviet government in Moscow was not pleased by Dubcek, nor were any of the puppet governments in any of the other Eastern Bloc countries, who could easily imagine their own people rising up to demand what the Czechoslovakians were receiving. By April, Soviet troops were beginning to mass on the Czechoslovakian border, even as leaders from Poland, Hungary, Bulgaria, and East Germany were advising Dubcek to make his socialism's face a little less human.

No country had ever overthrown its communist leadership. Hungarians had tried to do so in 1956, but the Soviets had quickly and brutally put an end to that experiment. Perhaps Dubcek believed the world wouldn't let the Soviets roll into his country and crush his "Prague Spring." At any rate, he refused to give in. By mid-August, several hundred thousand troops from all the Eastern Bloc countries were waiting on the border for the command to invade. On August 21st, the order came, and three days later, the Prague Spring was over.

Jaromir Jagr's grandmother raised him on tales of the thousands of people who took to the streets of Prague to stop the Soviet tanks with words, arguments, recrimination, and shame. She told him how people stripped the city of its street signs and house numbers so the KGB agents would not be able to find the homes of the most notorious liberals and artists. And she told him about another Jaromir Jagr—her husband and young Jaromir's grandfather. He first got in trouble with the Communists in 1948, when they took his farm as part of the collectivization of the country. He wound up spending three years in prison for his refusal to turn over his land. Then he was one of the thousands arrested in the aftermath of the Prague Spring of 1968. He died later that year, in prison.

The effect those stories had on Jagr is immediately obvious when you see him playing hockey. There is no other player who wears number 68, not even any of the other Czechs or Slovaks in the NHL. And it was those stories that implanted in him the burning desire to come to the United States. Bound up in the saga of the brief Czechoslovakian flowering of 1968 is another point of national pride that was not lost on Jagr. That was also the year that the Czechs played the Russians in the world hockey championships. The Czechs beat the Russians and people went crazy, Jagr said.

Jagr did not grow up in Prague but in Kladno, a small town not far from the capital. His mother and father both worked, leaving him in the care of his grandmother. "My parents worked on the farm and the factory so she spent all the time with me," Jagr said. "She told me all the stories about my grandfather and when she was younger and when the Communists were there, what they did. That's why I picked the number 68. He died in 1968. In jail he was living."

Growing up, Jagr always had the stories his grandmother told him to compare with the his-

As a student, Jaromir Jagr admired the United States and carried a picture of President Ronald Reagan in his wallet.

tory lessons given him by his teachers in school. And when he heard the official versions of what happened in 1968, of what Communist rule had done for his country, he took them for what they were. "They would tell us that the biggest opponent was the USA, that America was bad," he said. "All lies."

Jagr's pro-American feelings were so strong, he started carrying a photograph of then–U.S. President Ronald Reagan in his school books. It hardly seems like an act of rebellion to an American, but just as Reagan had labeled the Soviet Union "the Evil Empire," so the Communist regimes of Eastern Europe saw Reagan and the United States as their most threatening enemy.

"It was illegal," Jagr said. "You know how if something is illegal you want to do it? It was something for the people. The people who knew the truth."

Years later, when Reagan heard that Jagr risked jail to carry his photograph, the former president telephoned the young hockey star to thank him for the tribute. Jagr at first thought the call was a prank of his teammates, who, like Reagan, had read of the incident in a magazine article. "This is President Reagan?" Jagr responded. "Sure, and I am George Bush."

By a strange coincidence, Jagr would discover one of his first hockey idols in a player who would be his future teammate. In 1985, the World Junior Championships were held in Prague. The 13-year-old Jagr was too young to compete, but he watched from the stands, dazzled by the performance of a 19-year-old Canadian named Mario Lemieux. "Unbelievable," Jagr said of the memory. "Nobody could take the puck from him."

Jagr immediately decided that Lemieux was the player he would model himself after, and that same quality that struck the teenager in Prague, would 10 years later strike defensemen and opposing coaches all across North America.

Jagr showed an early talent for hockey, but his struggles with authority did not stop when he walked out the schoolroom door. When he started playing on the Kladno junior league team in 1986, his coaches would not let him wear his hair long, but what was worse, they would not permit him to wear the number 68. Rather than give in completely, Jagr etched the number into the side of his helmet.

If the coaches didn't like Jagr's view of history, they couldn't help but like the way he played the game of hockey. In 30 games that first year, Jagr scored 35 goals and added 35 assists. In 35 games the next season, he rifled in 57 goals and still managed to find a way to contribute 27

At age 18, Jagr was good enough to play for the Czech national team. Here he skates with the puck at the 1991 Canada Cup.

assists.

He had learned from what he saw Lemieux do. Just as the young Canadian was blazing a trail in North America by combining the finesse and precision of a Wayne Gretzky with the size and strength of the most physical defenseman, so Jagr was slashing through the ranks of Czech hockey. From watching Lemieux, Jagr found the inspiration to create a driving, full-throttle style that arose from his rare combination of size, strength, and speed.

He was promoted to Kladno's senior team when he was just 16, and though he struggled through an up-and-down first season, he came into his own in his second year, when he led the team in goals with 30 and was second in assists, also with 30. What really drew the attention of scouts from the NHL, though, was the 18-year-old's performances in the World Junior Tournament and the World Championships. Scouts had seen him beating up on his fellow Czechoslovakians, but for the first time they saw clearly that no one—not the skilled Russians, the rugged Swedes or Finns, not even the best of the young North American players who came closest to combining the best of the world's styles—could contain him. Czechoslovakia didn't win, but Jagr was the second-highest scorer in the Juniors with 18 points, earning a spot on the all-tournament team.

It didn't hurt Jagr's chances of attracting the interest of the NHL that in 1989, the Iron Curtain had started to come down. The so-called Velvet Revolution in Czechoslovakia had deposed the Communists, and scouts were scouring Eastern Europe for new talent. Jagr was the bright-

est—and one of the youngest—of the stars, and
it was clear his dream of playing in the NHL was
going to become a reality. The only question was,
who would take him.

THE EUROPEAN INVASION

Looking around the NHL in the late 1990s, it's hard to imagine a time when the talent of Eastern Europeans was ever questioned. Russians Pavel Bure, Aleksandr Mogilny, and Sergei Fedorov are perennial scoring leaders, and all across the league rosters are thick with the names of Swedes, Finns, Czechs, and Slovaks. But that was not always the case. Despite the dominance of the Soviet Union in Olympic and international hockey, North American players viewed Europeans as soft—all flash and no guts. Sure, their adults were able to beat up on Canadian and American kids in the Olympics, but they wouldn't have the strength or the toughness to make it in the NHL.

That perception started to change in 1972, the year of Jagr's birth. That was when a Canadian

In 1972, the best Canadian and Soviet hockey players squared off in the "Summit Series." Canada expected an easy win, but the Russians proved to be formidable opponents. Here Gary Bergman tries to defend against an onrushing Eugeny Mishakov.

In his first year as an NHL player, Jagr helped the Penguins win a Stanley Cup. He had five assists in the 1992 finals series against the Minnesota North Stars—a rookie record.

team of NHL all-stars and the Soviet national team played an eight-game series, known as the 1972 Summit Series. It was the first time that the best in the NHL would get a chance to show just how much better they were than the Soviets.

The Canadians approached the series as if it would be a romp. What they found was that they couldn't keep up with the Soviets. Canada won just one of the first five games, and managed to escape the series with a 4–3–1 edge only when Paul Henderson scored the game-winning goal in the eighth contest with just 34 seconds left.

Three of Canada's four victories were by a single goal, hardly the thrashing the North Americans expected to hand their opponents.

At that time, there was little thought of Eastern Europeans coming to play in the NHL. The Cold War was still raging, with sport as one of the most visible and socially acceptable battlefields. But the Summit got people on both sides of the Iron Curtain thinking. Fans found themselves enjoying the Russian style. It was less about hitting and more about skating. While the prevailing style in the NHL at the time was dump-and-chase, where you sent the puck into your opponent's end, then tried to beat him to it or, even better, fought him off it to get yourself in a position to score, the Russians preferred to carry the puck, using brilliant stick-handling to befuddle defensemen. When the puck left a Russian's stick, it was because he was sending it to a teammate.

The NHL had encouraged the hitting, dump-and-chase game by making its rinks smaller than the rinks for the international game. The bigger ice gave the better skaters an advantage, while the tighter rinks favored goons, the burly players who built their careers on their ability to slam opponents into the boards. Teams like the Philadelphia Flyers, known as "the Broad Street Bullies," reveled in their reputation for being hard hitters, but the line between a clean check and a cheap shot was becoming more and more blurry.

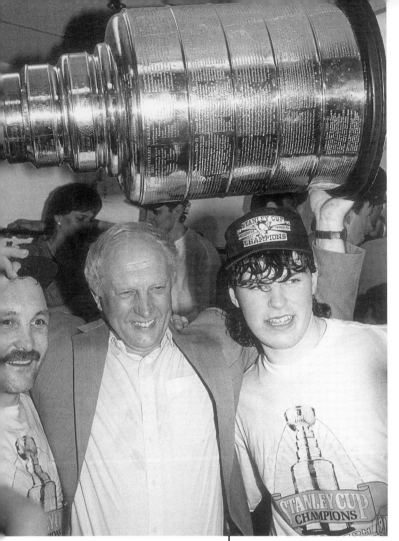

Jaromir Jagr's dad got to hoist the Stanley Cup in the celebrations after the final game. On the left is Bryan Trottier, who had helped the New York Islanders establish a champion dynasty during the early 1980s.

Fans were not the only ones impressed by the fluid Soviet style, which almost resembled basketball in its reliance on passing and lack of contact. North American coaches began encouraging players to develop their passing, puck handling, and skating skills, signaling the beginning of the end for the dump-and-chase. A seed was planted in the minds of Europeans as well. If the Russian team could play the Canadians to a virtual standoff, perhaps they could play in the NHL.

The impact was slow to be felt. A Swede named Borje Salming signed with Toronto for the 1973–74 season and wound up lasting 16 years with the Maple Leafs, scoring 768 career points. But it wasn't until the 1980s that the doors really started to open. Two Czechs, brothers Peter and Anton Stastny, defected in 1980 to join the Quebec Nordiques, and their brother Marian followed a year later. Swedes Stefan Persson, Tomas Jonsson, and Anders Kallur were prominent on the New York Islanders' Stanley Cup–winning teams from 1980 to 1984, and when the Edmonton Oilers reigned over the NHL in the mid-1980s, it was in large part due to Finns Jarri Kurri and Esa Tikkanen, whose flashy style blended well with the puck-handling and passing skills of Canadians Wayne Gretzky and Mark Messier.

Still, in 1989, when the collapse of Communism throughout Eastern Europe opened the door to a whole new world of hockey talent, some in the NHL remained unconvinced that Europeans could ever play a major role in North American hockey. The Soviet Union allowed some of its older stars to come play in the NHL for the 1989–90 season, looking for an infusion of cash into a struggling sports machine that had been hurt by the country's economic woes. Most of the players the Russians allowed to leave—in return for fees paid to the national hockey federation—were a disappointment in North America.

One Russian player who did live up to the expectations was the 19-year-old Mogilny, who defected to play for Buffalo and became an instant star. He had all the skills and quickness that NHL executives were expecting from the older Russians, and his brilliant rookie season had coaches and general managers eager to find young Russians of their own to add spark to their teams.

When the 1990 draft rolled around, it was not yet clear what would happen if you drafted a player from one of the former Eastern Bloc countries. And while Jagr was considered to be one of the potential prizes in the crop of players available, there were also rumors that Jagr wouldn't be allowed to leave his country until after the 1992 Olympics.

Five players had captured the imagination of the NHL in what was believed to be one of the richest drafts in recent years. Besides Jagr, there were Owen Nolan, Keith Primeau, Mike Ricci—

all Canadians who had been scouted almost since the time they first picked up a stick—and Petr Nedved and Jagr, two Czechs. Nedved had been playing in Canada since January 1989, when he defected after being the leading scorer at a junior tournament in Calgary, Alberta. Nedved had scored 32 goals in just 20 games for Litvinov before he defected, and then he earned the Canadian Major Junior Hockey Rookie of the Year award after scoring 65 goals and contributing 80 assists in 71 games with Seattle in 1989–90. The only unknown in the draft was Jagr, the mop-headed 18-year-old who had no experience playing North American–style hockey. But he was the player the Pittsburgh Penguins, who had the number five pick, had their eyes on.

The top four teams, Quebec, Vancouver, Detroit, and Philadelphia, all played it safe, going with the players who knew the North American game—and who they knew would be available. Yet, there was Jagr, with his parents, at the draft, the first player from Eastern Europe to attend without having to defect first. If that wasn't a sign that Jagr was committed to the NHL, the Penguins didn't know what was, and they couldn't believe their luck when he was still around for them to take with the fifth pick.

"We knew we were going to get one of those five," Pittsburgh general manager Craig Patrick said after the draft. "One of them was going to fall to us. We were hoping it was Jagr. We'd done some checking and we were convinced that he wanted to play in the NHL as soon as possible. In fact, immediately."

Jagr couldn't believe his luck either. Not only was his dream of playing in the NHL coming true, but he was going to the team where his idol, the great Mario Lemieux, played.

The Penguins brought Jagr and his parents to Pittsburgh the very next day, hoping to convince him to stay for the summer, to get used to life in the United States before training camp began in the fall—and secretly trying to avoid any possibility of the Czechoslovakian authorities keeping him from returning to America. But Jagr wanted to go back to Czechoslovakia to see his sister and say good-bye to his friends.

The Czechoslovakian hockey federation was still hoping Jagr would play for the national team in that summer's Goodwill Games in Seattle, yet the squad arrived in the United States without its young star. Czech newspapers said he had stayed behind to catch up on schoolwork. Insiders knew better. Veteran Czech center Jiri Hrdina remembered seeing the stories and feeling certain he knew exactly where Jagr was, and if Jagr was studying, then the textbooks were in English, not Czech. Indeed, Jagr and his mother, Anna, had driven across the border into Germany a few days before the Czech Goodwill Games team was supposed to head to Seattle. Jagr and his mother boarded a flight from Frankfurt to the United States, but its destination was not the Pacific Northwest. It was Pittsburgh.

As much as Jagr wanted to play in the NHL and live in the United States, he found the transition surprisingly difficult. True, he became one of just a handful of players in NHL history to score a goal in their first period on the ice, but Jagr's true mood soon began to show in his play. Despite a summer of seven-hour-a-day English classes that the Penguins had enrolled him in, he was still extremely uncomfortable with the language, and no matter how good he felt on the ice, off it he felt isolated. His mother had gone back to Kladno, leaving him with no ties to the country he found he loved more than he ever knew. Even with his teammates, he did not always find it easy to be comfortable. Lemieux was like a god to him, leaving the shy teenager tongue-tied, and he understood little of the culture around him

More than anything, he was homesick. Jagr's eagerness to play in the NHL was not because he didn't like Czechoslovakia, but because he wanted to play against the best in the world. True, he bristled at the refusal of Czech coaches to let him grow his hair long or to break a tradition that says hockey players cannot wear a number higher than 30 to let him put the number 68 on his jersey. He saw those things as a result of the Communist rule that was imposed on his country, a country whose true spirit was shown in the flowering of culture of the Prague Spring.

The Penguins were quick to notice their young star's blues, and in December, before his rookie season was half old, they took steps to make him a little more comfortable. In a swap of players that outside the Penguins locker room appeared virtually meaningless, Pittsburgh sent defenseman Jim Kyte to Calgary for Hrdina. Hrdina hadn't made a big impression in the NHL, but he was a former captain of the Czech national team. If nothing else, now Jagr would have somebody to talk to. As it turned out, the journeyman's contribution to the Penguins' future was immeasurable.

"I don't know what I would have done that year without him," Jagr said.

The change was noticeable almost immediately. Jagr says he plays better when he is happy, and having Hrdina around made him happy. He had someone to translate for him, someone who knew his way around the league, and most importantly, he had someone with whom he could reminisce about Czechoslovakia.

What it meant on the ice was that Jagr suddenly started playing the way the Penguins had hoped he could. In February, he became the youngest Penguin ever to score a hat trick, when he tallied three goals in a game against Boston. He finished the regular season with 27 goals and 30 assists, making the All-Rookie team. And 37 of his 57 points came in the second half of the season. In the playoffs, he showed more than just flash. He scored a game-winning goal in overtime against the New Jersey Devils in the first round—just the kind of thing Europeans weren't supposed to have the heart for—and led all rookies with 13 points in the playoffs.

Jagr still took a back seat to Lemieux, who almost single-handedly brought the Penguins back when they trailed New Jersey three games to two in the opening round, and the team's other established stars. But his NHL rookie-record five assists in the Stanley Cup finals against Minnesota were a big reason why the Penguins, after failing to even make the playoffs the year before, won the championship. For Jagr, though, even with playing a key role on a championship–winning team in his first season, things were still far from perfect.

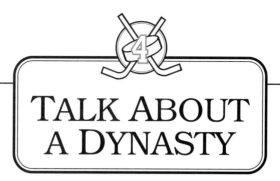

TALK ABOUT
A DYNASTY

Despite the on-ice success of his rookie season, Jagr still had an uneasy relationship with the United States. He hated to lose, and was bitterly disappointed with himself when he didn't play well. The reality of the National Hockey League is that even good teams lose fairly often, and when Jagr couldn't make a difference he became frustrated.

Adding to that was his discomfort speaking English. He didn't like talking to the media, particularly television, because he thought his accent sounded bad and he didn't believe he could make himself understood. Reporters watched his sometimes out-of-control one-on-one game, then saw him pouting. Jagr could be glum even after victories if he felt he hadn't played up to his potential. The media saw the talent and the high draft pick and, used to the friendliness of most North American players, labeled him a prima donna.

Jagr played in fewer games than usual in 1992. A players' strike cancelled 10 days of play, and Jagr was also suspended 10 days for bumping a referee.

It didn't matter that Jagr was still just a teenager, and it didn't matter that his teammates and coaches didn't see him the way the media did. The Penguins defended him as an extraordinarily talented youngster struggling to make his way in a strange country, but Jagr felt the hostility of the press and withdrew even further.

"My first year, I didn't do anything," Jagr said later. "I sat home all the time."

Certainly, some of the other Penguins didn't quite know what to make of Jagr, but they knew how hard he worked in practice and in games, and that mattered more than his insecurities off the ice.

After the Stanley Cup celebrations, Jagr returned to Kladno for the summer, where he could relax and not struggle to meet the various expectations of fans, reporters, teammates, and coaches. When he came back for training camp in the fall he received the first shock of his young career. Penguins coach Bob Johnson was desperately ill with brain cancer. He would die before winter.

"Badger was best coach in my life," Jagr would say of Johnson. "He was number one."

Despite the loss of his mentor, Jagr seemed more comfortable in his second season. His English had improved dramatically, aided by a steady diet of American television, especially the sitcom "Married... with Children," which he credited as being his main language tutor. He started behaving more like a typical—if rich—American teenager. He bought a black Camaro that he liked to drive too fast. Penguins general manager Patrick had to talk to Jagr more than once about his speeding. "On the ice, on skates," Patrick told him, "go as fast as you like. But on the road there's no reason to race."

On the ice, Jagr did love to race. His 6'2" frame had filled out to 208 pounds, but he'd lost none of his quickness and he showed an astonishing ability to handle the stick with one hand while fighting off clutching defensemen with the other, never losing a step. Teammates even joked that he should practice with 100-pound dummies on his back, to simulate what he faced every game.

More often than not, Jagr made opponents look like the dummies. "He can carry a couple guys and walk around the net and still have control of the puck," Penguins defenseman Ulf Samuelsson said. "He is so strong. His legs could be the strongest pair of legs I have ever seen on a hockey player."

But even with all that strength and skill, the banging and grabbing he faced night in and night out started to get to him, especially when it seemed referees were turning a blind eye to the muggings he was suffering. One night in late January he cracked. The Washington Capitals were doing everything in their power, legal or not, to stop Jagr and Lemieux, and referee Ron Hoggarth wouldn't blow his whistle. Finally Jagr charged Hoggarth, bumping the veteran referee. The misconduct earned him a 10-game suspension from the league.

Lemieux joined Jagr in his criticism of the referee, and Jagr claimed Hoggarth told him during the game that he wouldn't penalize North American players for fouls against Europeans. League officials claimed they never heard Jagr's complaints, but word somehow got down to the referees that they were to treat everyone the same, whether the ref could pronounce the player's name or not.

Jagr's new-found comfort off the ice made him a major celebrity in Pittsburgh. When a radio station reported that Jagr liked a certain candy bar, the Penguins offices started received mountains of the sweets from fans who didn't want the young man to go hungry. Jagr even overcame his shyness about his accent well enough to do weather broadcasts on his favorite rock radio station. And when he and his teammates went out on the town, Jagr was never in need of change to indulge in his passion for video games. "There'll be 100 young girls giving him quarters to play," Penguin forward Rick Tocchet said. "They tell me, 'Get your own.'"

Living the life of a star didn't hurt Jagr's hockey at all, which may explain why all the attention Jagr received left his teammates more amused than resentful. Jagr practiced as hard as he played, and he played as hard as anyone on the team. If anything, he played too hard. With the puck on his stick, he would outrace even his own teammates toward the opponents' goal. That would leave him to battle defensemen and goalie on his own, without the benefit of another Penguin to pass to, or at least to draw the defense's attention.

The spring brought Jagr a firsthand look at the working of the capitalist system he was now living in. The players, tired of working without a contract and despairing that negotiations were ever going to bring a settlement, called a strike. It was the first walkout in the history of the NHL, but was nothing new in sports, and really only proved that hockey players were catching up to the times. By 1992, professional baseball and

football had both seen more than a decade of labor problems.

Sports had become a bigger business than anyone could have imagined during the 1980s, with both players and owners finding new ways of making money. For players the big money was in endorsements of everything from sporting goods to pantyhose. The owners found they could haul in cash by selling shirts, hats, sweatshirts, coffee cups—in fact, just about anything—with the team logo on it, and by controlling their own television broadcasts. All this complicated negotiations between players and owners. Each side wanted its share and then some. The players believed that since it was their name on a jersey that made it valuable, they should be compensated. The owners contended that the play-

Jagr was too much for the Chicago Blackhawks in the 1992 Stanley Cup Finals. The Penguins, after having swept the Boston Bruins, beat Chicago in four straight games.

ers were already paid a salary, and that was enough.

The strike lasted 10 days, during which time Jagr went home to the Czech Republic. He worked out with his friends on the national team and the local squad in Kladno, and when a deal was finally reached, he came back refreshed. In the time away, Jagr seemed to have a chance to catch his breath. Early on, he'd wanted to do everything too fast. After the strike, his game calmed down just a bit. He was still usually the fastest player on the ice, but he was learning how to make better use of his speed. As the sea-

Jagr (right) is jubilant after the Penguins won their second consecutive championship. Also celebrating are Bryan Trottier (at bottom), Mario Lemieux (at left), and Rick Tocchet (center).

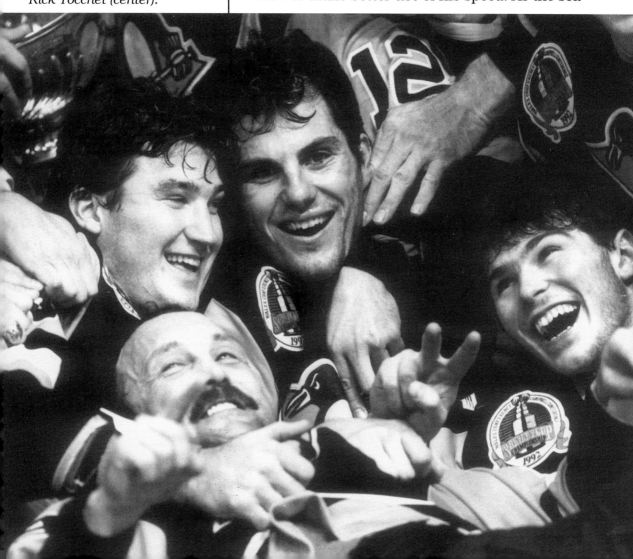

son wound down in May, he put together a nine-game stretch when he got at least a point in every contest—seven goals and eight assists.

Numbers don't always tell much about a player's true value, but in Jagr's case a couple of statistics stand out. In the 26 games when he scored at least one goal, the Penguins won 17 times, and of his 32 goals that season, 17 came in the third period, when most games are decided. With all the fun the young Czech was having off the ice, he was silencing all his critics with his play. Jagr was doing just what Europeans were not supposed to be able to do—come up big when the game was on the line

And the best was still yet to come. The Penguins finished third in the Patrick Division, but with the time off because of the strike, they seemed to have shaken off the black cloud that hung over them because of the death of Johnson. Scotty Bowman, who had come out of the front office to take over the team, finally had them playing like defending champions.

As he had in 1991, Lemieux carried Pittsburgh through the first round, with help from goaltender Tom Barrasso. The Washington Capitals led the series three games to one after a crushing 7–2 victory in Game 4 in Pittsburgh, but Lemieux could not be stopped in the final three games of the series.

The Rangers, though, found a way to stop him in the second round. Adam Graves broke his hand with a vicious slash that the Penguins claimed was intentional. What seemed to be a disaster for the Penguins only gave their youngest star the chance to shine. His game-winning performances in the final two contests of the brutal series lit up the hockey world.

As if to prove his performances against the Rangers were no fluke, Jagr got the Penguins started on a 4–0 sweep of Boston in the Wales Conference finals with an amazing overtime goal in Game 1, when Lemieux was still sidelined. Jagr swiped the puck from Bruins defenseman Don Sweeney, who was trying to get it out of Boston's end of the ice. Jagr eluded Sweeney's clawing to recover the puck, then tied rookie Matt Hervey in a knot to open his path to the goal.

"Every defense in the league is trying to figure out the right way to play Jagr," Boston coach Rick Bowness admitted. Bruins All–Star defenseman Ray Bourque, who missed the series with an injury but had a good seat on the sidelines, said simply, "Jagr is a human highlight film."

Lemieux came back for Game 2, and the Penguins rolled into the Stanley Cup championship against the Chicago Blackhawks, not losing another game. With Lemieux on the ice, Jagr took a backseat to the player now considered the greatest in the game, but Mario Jr. had his moments.

In the first game against the Blackhawks, the Penguins fell behind 4–1 at home against a team that had won 11 straight games. Rick Tocchet and Lemieux scored 59 seconds apart to bring Pittsburgh within a goal heading into the final period. Chicago held Pittsburgh scoreless for the first 15 minutes of the third period, and seemed ready to stretch their winning streak to 12 games before Jagr ignited the Penguins. He used his strength to battle out of the corner with the puck, eluded three Blackhawks on his way to the goal, then put the puck between the pads of the best goalie in the game at the time, Ed Belfour, to tie the score. Even Lemieux was impressed, calling it the greatest goal he had ever seen.

"That's the great thing about Jaromir," he said. "He has the ability to score unbelievable goals when you need them most. That's the mark of a great player."

That unbelievable goal seemed to break the spirit of the Blackhawks. Lemieux scored with 13 seconds left to give the Penguins the victory. They won Game 2 by limiting Chicago to just eight shots over the final 40 minutes, and shut out the Blackhawks 1–0 in Game 3. The Penguins' offense shone again in the final game, which Pittsburgh won 6–5.

The Penguins' second straight Stanley Cup championship had fans talking about a dynasty to match the great New York Islanders and Edmonton Oilers teams of the 1980s. The defense proved in the playoffs that it didn't deserve the criticism it had received all season, Barrasso was a top-notch goaltender, and not only did they have more good forwards than any other team in the league, they also had perhaps the best in the world and his heir-apparent, Super Mario and Mario Jr.

The summer brought another vacation in Kladno with his family and friends. In the Czech Republic, the lifting of Communist rule had opened doors to former dissidents to tell their stories, and writers who had fled the old regime were able to return, their books now published for their countrymen to finally read. Like so many Czechs, Jagr's appetite for these previously suppressed voices was voracious.

After living with an American family during the 1991–92 season, Jagr decided it was time to go out on his own—but not completely. He brought his mother, Anna, back to America with him when he returned to Pittsburgh for the start of the 1992–93 campaign. He rented an apartment for the two of them outside of the city.

Jagr's performance during the Penguins' astonishing run to the Stanley Cup the previous spring created incredible expectations for the young man entering his third season in the NHL. At an

No goalie—not even a hot John Vanbiesbrouck of the Rangers—can stop Jagr from point-blank range.

age when even the most talented hockey players are still toiling in the junior leagues or in college, Jagr was being compared to the greatest scorer in the game. And not all the comparisons were coming from breathless Penguins fans. For Jagr, though, having Lemieux sitting across the locker room from him, practicing against him, and playing alongside him was perhaps the best medicine against succumbing to the head-swelling that such praise could have caused.

"Mario's the best player in the world," Jagr said in response. "He means a lot to us. I look at him in practice and I know I can never be like him."

Of course Jagr had his critics. Unlike Lemieux, he was still not a great passer, and strangely, for all the brilliance of his one-on-one moves, he was not quite the scorer that it seemed he could be. It was as though Jagr mesmerized not only opposing defensemen with his puck handling, he sometimes seemed to mesmerize himself. Instead of shooting when he had an opportunity, he would put on yet another move, stun another defenseman with his brilliant skating—but in the meantime, the opportunity to score was lost.

"I have to shoot more, but I never will," Jagr admitted midway through the season. "I don't know why. I was born like that. I want to do some moves all the time. I tell myself before games, 'You have to shoot more,' but when I go into a game and come into a situation to shoot it, I never shoot. I don't know why."

Never was too strong a word. Jagr managed to get the puck off his stick for 34 goals that season, ranking fourth on the team, and was credited with 60 assists. He also hadn't lost his abil-

ity to come up big. His nine game-winning goals was second only to Lemieux, who set a club record with 10 despite missing 24 games with back problems and Hodgkin's disease.

The Penguins' franchise-record 56-win, 21-loss, 7-tie season—which included an NHL record 17-game winning streak—was all the more remarkable because of all the distractions the team faced. When Lemieux was out, the Penguins' weaknesses showed. Eleven of their losses came with Super Mario sidelined. The suspect defense couldn't take the increased pressure it faced when opponents didn't have to worry about Lemieux. And without the reflected glare of Super Mario's brilliance shining on him, Jagr seemed to fade. For the first time in his career, Jagr started hearing criticisms he couldn't answer. People expected him to carry the Penguins with Lemieux out, the way he had against

In 1993, Jagr and the Penguins were ousted in the second round of the playoffs by the New York Islanders.

the Rangers in the playoffs the previous year.

Jaromir wasn't happy. Scotty Bowman, who had replaced Bob Johnson as the Penguins head coach, wasn't as impressed as his predecessor with the young Czech's skills. He took him off the first line, drastically cutting his playing time. Unlike Johnson, Bowman had little rapport with his players. He was the winningest coach in NHL history, and that should be enough to make any player accept his decisions without a second thought. Jagr, though, had never been one to blindly accept what an authority figure said. He heard the reaction he got from fans wherever he went. He knew what his teammates and opponents said about his skill, and he started to feel that the only thing holding him back was Bowman's refusal to use him. He had two years left on his contract, but he'd seen enough of professional sports in North America to know a contract was not a chain.

"In two years I won't be here," Jagr said before the playoffs began that spring, adding that he thought he might well be traded the following season. There were two clubs that were to start playing the following season—one in Miami and one in Anaheim, California. Those were new markets, in places with sunshine and beaches all year round. That sounded good to Jagr.

"The expansion is good for me and the other guys who want to play more," he said. "In two years I'll be scoring 150 points."

Even the prospect of leaving a Stanley Cup contender for a team that might struggle to win 25 games didn't seem to bother him. "I don't need more rings," he said of the jewelry that comes with winning a Stanley Cup. "I just need money and beaches and girls."

As for the Penguins management, they knew they could get a lot in return for Jagr if they decided to trade him. The question was, could any team possibly give enough? Jagr's boast about his potential did not seem to be too far from the truth some nights. Over and over, players, sportswriters, and coaches sang Jagr's praises. They said he was better than Eric Lindros, the young Canadian who sparked a $15 million bidding war between the New York Rangers and Philadelphia Flyers. They said he might be better than Lemieux had been in his third season.

He was unhappy, and he wanted out of Pittsburgh. Team president Howard Baldwin said, "It's not the first time I've heard that. We're not going to hold Jaromir prisoner." But taking a tip from their flashy young star, the Penguins kept the puck on their stick. Offers came fast and furious, but the Penguins refused to pull the trigger.

Even with all that, the Penguins racked up the best record in the league. When Lemieux made his surprising return in time for the playoffs, Pittsburgh became the overwhelming favorite to win a third straight Stanley Cup.

Things quickly fell apart in the playoffs, though. They defeated the New Jersey Devils, who had barely qualified for the postseason, in five games, but struggled against the upstart New York Islanders, eventually falling in seven games. The Penguins had been hailed as the best team in hockey all season, but it turned out to be a paper crown. The real trophy, Lord Stanley's Cup, went to the Montreal Canadiens.

HIGH SCORER

The next season it was Bowman who was gone, not Jagr. Blaming the coach is always an easy way out when a team fails to meet the expectations of fans, but in the Penguins' case it seemed to be a fitting response to the problem. Jagr wasn't the only player unhappy under Bowman's reign, which made it easier for general manager Craig Patrick to reject the coach's contract demands.

Replacing the icy Bowman was Eddie Johnston, the man who had drafted Lemieux a decade earlier. Like Bob Johnson, Johnston was a player's coach, and he had a vision of what the Penguins could be that Jagr and his teammates liked. Johnston wanted to take advantage of what was regarded as the best group of forwards in hockey by keeping his players moving when they didn't have the puck, to keep defenses off balance, and create more scoring chances. He

Balzano, Italy, was the site for the 1994 World Championships. Jagr suited up for the Czech Republic.

Kevin Klee and goalie Jim Carey are left sprawling as Jagr puts in a goal against the Washington Capitals during the 1995 playoffs.

wanted to see his defensemen more involved in the offense—a tactic imported to the Hockey League along with the rich crop of Russians.

It didn't hurt Jagr's mood that the Penguins had brought in another young Czech, Martin Straka, who was impressive in the preseason while Lemieux sat out resting his back. Straka and Jagr took neighboring lockers in the Penguins' dressing room. There was no more talk of trades to warmer, sunnier cities.

But there was little talk of dynasties, either. After off-season surgery, Lemieux could not overcome his back problems. He missed the first 10 games of the season and sat out a total of 58 during the regular season. For Jagr, the year was a revelation. For the first time he was forced to play night after night without his hero on the ice. Instead of wilting, though, Jagr stepped into Lemieux's skates and found they were a pretty good fit. He became the first European to lead the team in scoring, with 99 points, his best season so far, and ninth best in the league. He was named a starter in the All-Star Game, but was sidelined by an injury he suffered in the skills competition, which takes place the day before the annual showcase game.

Jagr lost his shyness about shooting, and even when Lemieux came back to the lineup for brief stints, Mario Jr. didn't take a back seat. He tried to make things as easy as possible on his idol. Opponents had started to believe that Jagr could be intimidated by rough physical play, and as his goal and assist numbers increased, so did the number of vicious checks he experienced at the elbows, shoulders, and hips of zealous defensemen.

But Jagr finally had what he'd said he wanted—ample playing time—and he was making the most of it. Lemieux's absence and the realignment of the NHL, which had put Pittsburgh in a division with the bruising Boston Bruins and Montreal Canadiens, was supposed to hurt the Penguins, but Jagr carried Pittsburgh to first place in the Northeast Division.

He couldn't carry them in the playoffs, though. Pittsburgh suffered its earliest loss since Jagr was drafted, falling in six games to the Washington Capitals. Jagr scored the game-winner in Game 5, when the Penguins faced elimination on their home ice, but Pittsburgh went quietly in Game 6 in Washington.

The season was seen as a good year for hockey, though. In his second year as commissioner, the former National Basketball Association executive Gary Bettman had presided over a marketing boom. Hockey jerseys were becoming part of the street fashion, even in cities where there were no teams. The growing popularity of in-line skate hockey had carried over to a growth in interest in the NHL, and the New York Rangers' first Stanley Cup championship in 54 years didn't hurt, either. Led by Mark Messier, a charismatic veteran who at times seemed to carry the Rangers to victory by the force of his will, the Broadway Blueshirts captured the imagination of the media capital. With young players like Jagr, Bure, Mogilny, and Lindros, the league had the marketable stars to bring it into competition with the NBA for the hearts of sports fans. Bettman cracked down on fighting and the goonish tactics that turned many people, particularly in the United States, away from the game. He'd learned from his years in pro basketball that what people wanted to see was great players taking it to the net. Hockey could have just as much of that as the NBA did.

The NHL's owners were ready to learn from the NBA, but the one lesson that they didn't get soon enough was that the fans won't come if you don't play the game. Still unable to come to a long-term contract with the players' union, the owners decided to lock them out before the start of the 1994–95 season. The issues were much the same as they had been a year and a half earlier, when the players staged their brief strike. The owners wanted a limit on how much teams would be allowed to pay their players, and they wanted control on players' rights to move from one team to another. The players wanted their freedom, and they wanted a bigger cut of the money the owners made from selling jerseys, T-shirts, and other merchandise.

Jagr was mostly just anxious to get back on the ice. Lemieux had announced before training camp was scheduled to begin that he would take the season off to try to make a full recovery from his back surgery and the lingering effects of Hodgkin's disease, which had left him weak even nearly two years after he was cured. When it started to seem that the season would never get under way, Jagr went to Europe. He played 10 games for his old team in the Czech professional league, and went to Italy for the World Cup, where he played five games. But after Christmas he went home to Kladno and took it easy.

Then, suddenly, in January, there was movement. Owners and players both started to

Mario Lemieux and "Mario Jr." hang out during a workout.

soften their stand. The owners set a deadline for an agreement to be reached if there was to be a season. It passed, but the owners agreed to another, final deadline. Before that one passed, the two sides came to an agreement. There would be a seven-day, mini-training camp, and then an abbreviated season would be played. Forty-eight games would be squeezed in before a full playoff schedule.

Jagr hurried back to Pittsburgh. He later admitted, "I was in the worst shape ever," but nobody in the NHL could tell. Lemieux was out for the year, and Jagr wasted no time laying his claim to the offensive leadership role that Super Mario had played. It quickly became apparent that Mario Jr. was going to need a new nickname. He kept the Penguins undefeated over their first 13 games, which they took at a 12–0–1 pace, and through Pittsburgh's first 21 contests Jagr had a phenomenal total of 16 goals and 17 assists. Among those was a blind backhand game-winner against the Quebec Nordiques that he got off after eluding two defensemen—despite having a Quebec forward trying to share his jersey even as he flipped the puck past the Nordiques' netminder. It was one of those goals that had fans shaking their heads in disbelief. Lemieux himself said it was "among the greatest goals he'd ever seen."

In 1995, Jagr won the NHL scoring title. Here Karl Dykhuis of the Philadelphia Flyers trips up Jagr, who nevertheless gets a shot off against goalie Dominic Roussel.

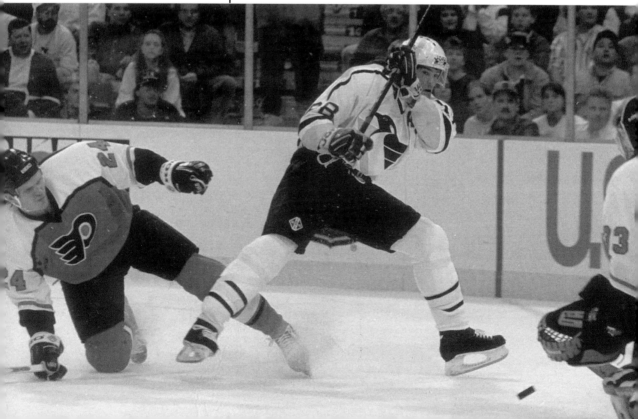

The Penguins had all but been counted out of contention, but almost single-handedly, Jagr was keeping them in the hunt. Just as it had been early in his career, one of Jagr's biggest boosters was his coach, who saw more to the player than long curly hair hanging down his back and flashy one-on-one play. "He knows the game better than anyone on the team," Johnston said. "He's very smart out there. He knows the little things, things you can't teach. He knows how to play the angles and how to protect the puck. You know where he got that don't you? From Mario."

Jagr would never deny that. Fittingly, Jagr had changed his life a bit off the ice as well. At the age of 23 he was suddenly a very rich man, having signed a five-year, $19.5 million contract, and was also homeowner. He got rid of his sports car for a four-wheeler that would be better able to deal with the winters in western Pennsylvania. He even found himself a steady girlfriend, whose name and face he somehow managed to keep secret from the inquisitive Pittsburgh media.

"When I was 18, I thought hockey was all that mattered," he said. "But no more. Now I know how important life is. Hockey is still great and a lot of fun and a great job, but it's not everything in my life. I used to think if I play a bad game, my life is over. Now I realize that if I play a bad game, well, so what? Life is still good."

That kind of thinking only helped Jagr to play fewer bad games. Instead of sulking after a poor performance, he was now able to leave the game behind him on the ice, where it belonged. The only thing he took with him off the ice were the bruises and cuts inflicted on him by defensemen, who had come to realize that if they were to have any hope of stopping him, they had to hit him with everything they had—legal or not.

The season didn't finish as well as it had begun for Pittsburgh. The absence of Lemieux caught up with them and by the end of the year they had slipped to second place in the Northeast Division. Jagr never lost a step though. In the final game of the season he recorded an assist that gave him 70 points and the Art Ross Trophy as the highest scorer in the league. He became the first player not named Lemieux or Gretzky to win the Ross since the 1979–80 season, and the first European ever to take the title.

At the awards dinner, Jagr obliterated any memories of the temperamental teenager who came into the league when he graciously said that Lindros, who also finished with 70 points but lost out because he scored only 29 goals to Jagr's 32, would have won the award had he not been injured for the final game of the season. He then went on to credit his teammates, saying that without good players beside you, you cannot win the scoring title.

With that speech, delivered in his quiet, still-accented English, Jagr proved himself worthy of the superstar status he had reached with his brilliant season. Jagr kept up his torrid pace in the postseason, scoring seven goals and adding four assists in the Penguins' seven-game first round series victory over Washington. They fell behind three games to one and were within a goal of losing in Game 5 before they rallied. A 7–1 victory in Game 6 and a series clinching 3–0 shutout in the seventh game gave the Penguins the right to meet the New Jersey Devils in the second round.

The Devils, who came within a goal of reaching the Stanley Cup finals the year before, were well rested, and they knew what their task was to stop Pittsburgh—stop Jagr. And New Jersey did just that. The Devils had the league's hottest goalie, Martin Brodeur, who had allowed less than one goal per game in New Jersey's first-round victory over Boston. They also played a defense-oriented style, smothering opponents and taking advantage of the mistakes their swarming created. The Penguins pulled out the first game when Luc Robitaille scored with 1:16 left in the game, but they did not manage another victory. In the final three games, the Penguins scored a total of just three goals. Their only consolation was that New Jersey went on to win the Cup.

Jagr poses with the Art Ross trophy, awarded him as the high scorer in 1995.

Lemieux's return the following season did not take the spotlight off Jagr. Lemieux was again the team captain, with Jagr and Ron Francis serving as alternates, but now Lemieux benefited as much from the attention defenses paid Jagr as the 23-year-old Czech did from the presence of his older teammate. Jagr still cherished the company of Czech teammates, and the Penguins' decision to trade Straka, his best friend on the team, hurt him. When reporters asked

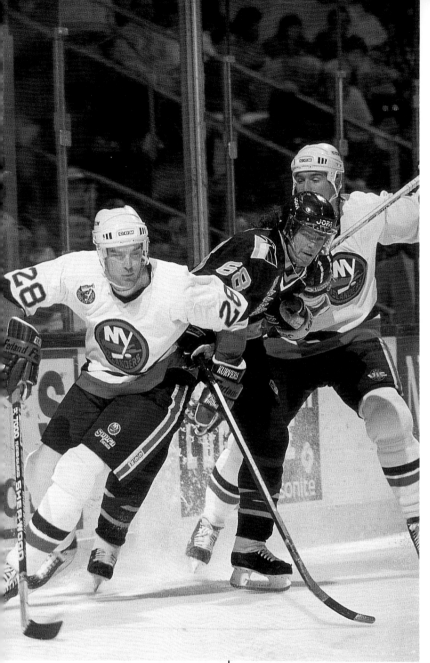

Jagr has to get used to the idea of two defensemen covering him—and occasionally battering him—wherever he goes.

him how he felt about the deal, he could not hold back tears, even though he said he understood that hockey was a business.

Johnston had spoken to Jagr about the deal before it was done, and he and Patrick quickly brought in another Czech who they hoped would more than fill Straka's skates—Petr Nedved. The player taken second overall the year Jagr went fifth had found the NHL a rougher road than his countryman. He was never happy in Vancouver, and sat out most of 1993–94, playing for the Canadian national team and scoring five goals in eight games for the silver-medal winning Canadian Olympic team at Lillehammer, Norway. After the Olympics he signed with the St. Louis Blues, but was shipped to New York in the offseason. Nedved never fit in with the Rangers, who thought he was soft. Though Messier never said it directly, the New York press reported that the Ranger captain did not like

Czechs, believing that their national spirit had been crushed by years of Soviet domination.

The Penguins were able to grab Nedved and young Russian defenseman Sergei Zubov for two aging players, Luc Robitaille and Ulf Samuelsson. It was a deal that would come back to haunt New York.

Jagr's coming of age in the year Lemieux was away meant that the older man would now find competition for a scoring title coming from one of own teammates, but there was no question of there being hard feelings between the two. Lemieux said he was looking forward to the challenge from a player he knew idolized him. As for Jagr, he had already made quite clear what he felt his relationship to Lemieux was. When he was on his way to the scoring trophy the year before, reporters had hounded him with questions about how it felt to be replacing Lemieux. Jagr's English might not have been perfect, but he knew enough to correct them on that count. Lemieux was not a player who could be replaced. He was the greatest in the game, and Jagr? Well, he was just trying to do his best, trying to play hard every night.

Even with Lemieux back, and Jagr pushed back onto the second line, he had no more complaints about playing time. Johnston gave almost equal shifts to the first and second lines, and he used Jagr on the first line when the Penguins were playing on the power play and kept him on the ice in most penalty-killing situations as well. Jagr found himself in the new position of being a role model for other players, some of them barely younger than himself. Though he was just 23 at the start of the season, he already had two Stanley Cup rings and the Art Ross Trophy, not to mention having been runner-up for the Hart Trophy for most valuable player. Young players on the Penguins liked it that he was their age, so he could relate to them better than the older stars, but he had just as much to share as the veterans did.

He and Lemieux did lead the way in the scoring race. Through 17 games, Lemieux had 17 goals and 24 assists for 41 points, while Jagr had 16 goals and 21 assists for 37. After 47 games, Lemieux had 42 goals and 62 assists, giving him 104 points. Jagr was still second best at 40, 54, and 94.

All the fire-power was keeping the Penguins on top of the Northeast Division, a position they would hold right up to the end of the season. Lemieux won the scoring title, but Jagr set a record for most points by a European player and kept up his role as the big-goal scorer. He led the team with 12 game-winners, and his teammates credited him with many more than that. When a player scored the kind of goals Jagr scored, astonishing plays where he would undress a couple defensemen and the goalie before putting the puck into the net, it played with a team's mind. Fans might leap to their feet and roar at the kind of goals Jagr scored—even in cities other than Pittsburgh—but they made opponents' hearts drop.

The Penguins entered the 1996 Stanley Cup playoffs as one of the favorites again. Their defense was still questioned, though Zubov had finally matured into the player the Rangers had hoped he could be—a goal-scorer whose defense didn't suffer from his love of playing in the opponents' end of the ice.

Pittsburgh dispatched the Washington Capitals despite having lost the first two games at home. Lemieux struggled in the series, but Jagr and Nedved were both brilliant. The fourth game was a six hour, 27-minute marathon that lasted into the fourth overtime before Nedved won it for Pittsburgh with 44 seconds left, scoring his second goal of the game. That contest was the first time Lemieux had been thrown out of a game in his career. Maybe it was frustration at his inability to score a goal, but Lemieux broke out in Game 5, which Pittsburgh won easily.

In Game 6, Lemieux and Jagr had both scored before the contest was seven minutes old, and after Ron Francis added a third goal 13 minutes into the first period, the Penguins held on to win the series four games to two. Pittsburgh's second-round matchup turned out to be with the New York Rangers. Jagr still held a grudge against them because of what they had done to Lemieux in the 1992 series, and both Zubov and Nedved read the negative things their former teammates and coaches said about them. It didn't help that New York coach Colin Campbell belittled the Penguins before the series began, saying they didn't compare to the 1992 team, and hinting that Jagr and Nedved wouldn't be able to take the pounding the Rangers were ready to dish out.

The trouble was, the Rangers found they couldn't catch Jagr. There were plenty of cheap shots from the Rangers, the Penguins would claim, and plenty of acting from the Penguins, the Rangers would say. One brilliant performance came from Nedved, who writhed on the ice after being slashed by Messier. The Ranger captain was sent to the penalty box, and with a man advantage on the ice, Jagr took a perfect pass from Zubov on the fly and beat Rangers goalie Mike Richter, then put Pittsburgh up 2–0 by outracing a New York defenseman and again taking Richter one-on-one.

The Rangers rallied to take the lead 3–2, before Dave Roche tied the score for Pittsburgh. Then Jagr and Lemieux teamed up for the game–winner. Jagr, who was seeing double-duty in the game, was supposed to be heading to the bench for a line change and a much needed rest, when he found himself with the puck at center ice and Ranger defenseman Bruce Driver trying to check him. Jagr went around Driver like the defender was a statue, and Lemieux, catching scent of the goal, was suddenly racing along with him. Jagr let New York's lone defenseman Brian Leetch see his eyes focus on the net, then fed the streaking Lemieux for a backdoor goal.

"He wasn't still supposed to be out there on that play, but it's hard to get him off the ice," Lemieux said.

Messier took on the task of stopping Lemieux in Game 2, and the Rangers' physical tactics worked, giving New York a 5–3 victory. Robitaille answered criticism from Zubov by scoring a goal, but two of Pittsburgh's three tallies came with Robitaille in the penalty box and the Penguins on the power play. Pittsburgh scored three goals in the first 15 minutes of Game 3, and Penguins goalie Ken Wregget came up big to hold on to the victory.

In Game 4, Jagr silenced Madison Square Garden with a goal just four minutes into the game. He scooped up a loose puck deep on the right side, and rather than skating out for a better angle, let fire a shot that snuck just inside the far post. Again, Wregget was key in helping the Penguins hold on, stopping 40 shots. Perhaps frustrated by the failure of the strong-arm tactics, the Rangers continued to criticize the Penguins, saying they were drawing penalties by flopping to the ice whenever a New Yorker so much as breathed heavily on them.

Jagr and Lemieux responded the best way they knew how. In Game 5, with a chance to close out the series in front of their home fans, Jagr and Lemieux both scored hat tricks to give Pittsburgh a 7–3 win. The Rangers, built in the old school mode of bruisers and intimidators, couldn't hit what they couldn't catch.

Jagr is a favorite with Penguins fans. Here he autographs a hockey stick at a Make-A-Wish children's party.

There wasn't a Stanley Cup in the Penguins' future, though. What the Rangers couldn't achieve with brawn, the Florida Panthers accomplished with speed, relentless defensive pressure, and superb goaltending. By shadowing Lemieux and Jagr whenever they were on the ice, Florida managed to force the Penguins to look to their other players for scoring. They didn't provide enough attacking power to make the Panthers change their strategy, and Florida prevailed in seven games.

Lemieux announced that the 1996-97 season would be his last, and while he had another terrific season, the Penguins were only as good as their younger star. Jagr started off hot, scoring 41 goals in the first 44 games. But a groin injury hampered him for nearly two months. Pittsburgh had a fine record of 33-22-5 when Jagr played a full game. Otherwise, the team could only muster a 5-14-3 record.

The Penguins' sixth place finish pitted them against the Philadelphia Flyers in the first round of the playoffs. "They're going to try to beat the heck out of me," said Jagr. "I've got to figure out how to deal with it." Mario, playing in his last playoffs, and Jaromir tried to spark the Penguins, but the Flyers were too strong and too fast. Philadelphia went on to the Stanley Cup finals, while Pittsburgh went home to plan for next year.

Still, at the tender age of 25, Jagr had established himself as one of the greatest players in the game. Blessed with speed and stickhandling ability few players could match, Jagr also learned to look for his teammates, to use his talent to create opportunities for those around him. More than anything, he had earned the respect of a man he once said was like a god to him.

STATISTICS

Season	Team	Regular Season					Playoffs				
		GP	G	A	PTS	PIM	GP	G	A	PTS	PIM
1990-91	Pitt	80	27	30	57	42	24	3	10	13	6
1991-92	Pitt	70	32	37	69	34	21	11	13	24	6
1992-93	Pitt	81	34	60	94	61	12	5	4	9	23
1993-94	Pitt	80	32	67	99	61	6	2	4	6	16
1994-95	Pitt	48	32	38	70	37	12	10	5	15	6
1995-96	Pitt	82	62	87	149	96	18	11	12	23	18
1996-97	Pitt	63	47	48	95	40	5	4	4	8	4
Totals		504	266	367	633	371	98	46	52	98	79

GP	games played
G	goals
A	assists
PTS	points
PIM	penalty minutes

JAROMIR JAGR
A CHRONOLOGY

1972   Born on February 15, in Kladno, Czechoslovakia.

1984   Sees Mario Lemieux playing in Junior Tournament in Prague.

1986   Begins play in Kladno Junior team in the Czech League.

1988   Promoted to Kladno senior team.

1990   Leads Kladno in scoring with 60 points in 51 games; is second-leading scorer in World Junior Tournament in Helsinki; taken number five overall by Pittsburgh Penguins in the National Hockey League draft; leaves Czechoslovakian Goodwill Games team to come to Pittsburgh and prepare for NHL.

1991   At age 18, becomes youngest player in Penguins history to score three goals in a game, recording his first NHL hat trick against Boston; is named to NHL All-Rookie team, and sets a Stanley Cup finals record for most assists by a rookie with five versus Minnesota.

1992   Suspended for 10 games for bumping referee Ron Hoggarth, who Jagr said told him he would not call penalties on North American players fouling Europeans; has a nine-game scoring streak, which included first ever penalty shot goal by a Penguin in the playoffs; helps Penguins repeat as Stanley Cup champions.

1993   Suffers a separated shoulder and misses three games, but goes on to set a career high for goals with 34.

1994   Becomes first non-Canadian to lead Pittsburgh in scoring with 99 points. Finishes season on nine-game scoring streak. In January is voted to start for the East in the NHL All-Star game, but suffers a groin injury in the skills competition and has to sit out.

1995   Becomes first European, and first player since 1979 other than Wayne Gretzky or Mario Lemieux, to win Art Ross trophy as league's leading scorer; finishes second to Eric Lindros as league's most valuable player.

1996   Breaks Mike Bossy's records for points and assists by a right wing and breaks Peter Stastny's record for points by a European with his 62 goals, 87 assists, and 149 points.

SUGGESTIONS FOR FURTHER READING

Callahan, Gerry. "Looming Large." *Sports Illustrated*, March 13, 1995.

Coffey, Phil. "Jagr-Mania Spreads Like Wild Fire!" *Superstar Hockey Yearbook 1992/93.*

Diamond, Dan, editor. *The Official National Hockey League Stanley Cup Centennial Book.* Buffalo: Firefly Books, 1992.

Fischler, Stan. *Fischler's Illustrated History of Hockey.* Toronto: Warwick Publishing, 1993.

Gave, Keith. "Unleashed from the East." *The Sporting News 1992–93 Hockey Yearbook.*

Grove, Bob. "And You Thought the Penguins were Done." *Hockey Digest,* Summer 1995.

Grove, Bob. "Popular Penguin," *Beckett Hockey,* February 1993.

McMillan, Tom. "The Americanization of Jaromir Jagr." *The Sporting News 1995–96 Hockey Yearbook*

McMillan, Tom. "Kit Kat Kid Perfectly Popular in Pittsburgh." *Inside Hockey,* February/March 1993.

McMillan, Tom. "Mario is Back, but He Can't Carry the Penguins." *The Sporting News 1995–96 Hockey Yearbook.*

Sullivan, Matt. "Europeans Discover Success in a Brave, New World." *Hockey Illustrated, 1992–93.*

Thomson, Lois. "Disappointing Loss Brings Jagr to Penguins." *Penguins Magazine, 1995–96.*

Ulmer, Michael. Jaromir Jagr: "The Elusive One." *The Hockey News,* February 9, 1996.

ABOUT THE AUTHOR

Dean Schabner has been a sportswriter with United Press International since 1989. In that time he has covered the NHL, the NBA, and the hockey championships at the 1994 Olympics in Lillehammer, as well as the 1996 Olympics in Atlanta. He was educated at Reed College and Boston University.

INDEX